SCHIRMER'S LIBRARY
OF MUSICAL CLASSICS

Vol. 2101

WOLFGANG AMADEUS MOZART

Favorite Piano Works

7 Sonatas
2 Sets of Variations
Rondo in D Major, K. 485
Sonatina in C Major
Fantasia in D minor, K. 397

ISBN 978-1-4768-7554-5

G. SCHIRMER, *Inc.*

DISTRIBUTED BY

HAL•LEONARD®
CORPORATION
7777 W. BLUEMOUND RD. P.O. BOX 13819 MILWAUKEE, WI 53213

www.musicsalesclassical.com
www.halleonard.com

CONTENTS

RONDO
in D Major

Wolfgang Amadeus Mozart
K. 485

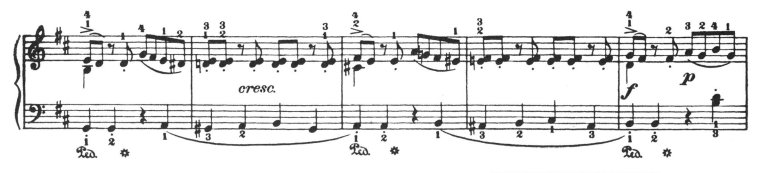

PIANO SONATA
in F Major

Edited, revised and fingered by
Richard Epstein

Wolfgang Amadeus Mozart
K. 332

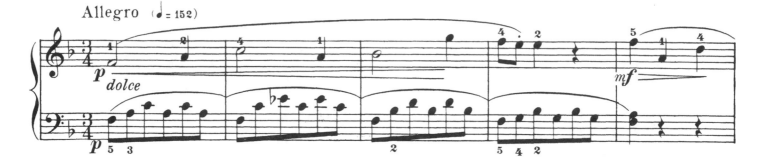

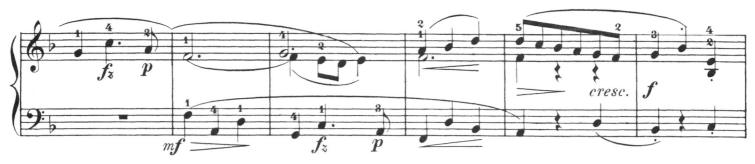

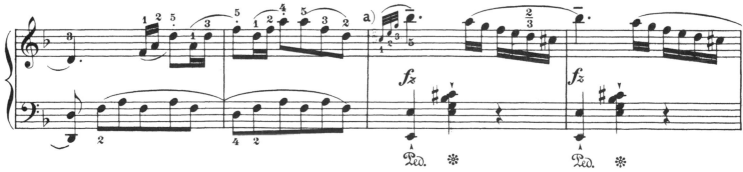

poco marcato

a)

15

Adagio (♪ = 84)

a)

Allegro assai (♩.= 96)

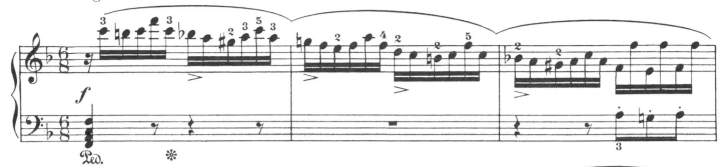

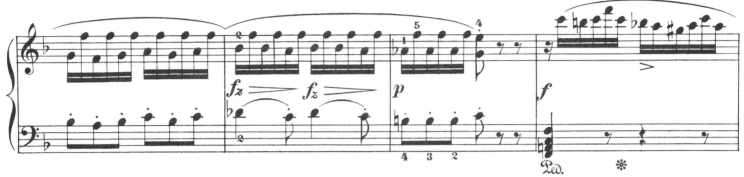

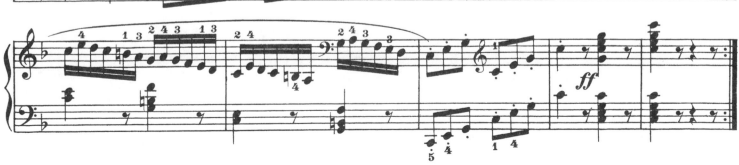

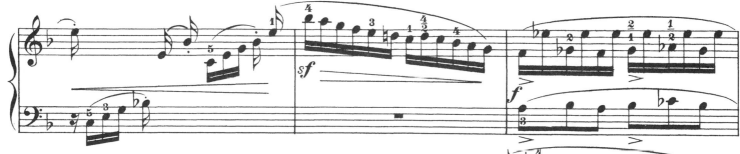

25

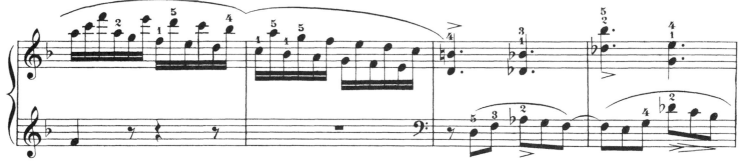

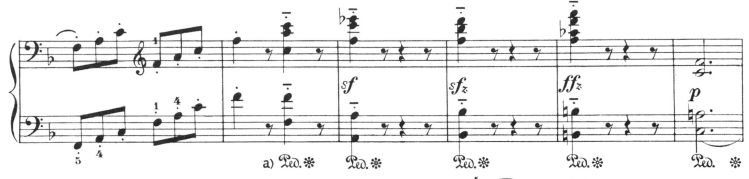

a) Ped. ✳ Ped. ✳ Ped. ✳ Ped. ✳ Ped. ✳

Ped. ✳ Ped. ✳

a) Keep the pedal very short each time, *quasi staccato*.

PIANO SONATA
in C Major

Edited, revised and fingered by
Richard Epstein

Wolfgang Amadeus Mozart
K. 545

29

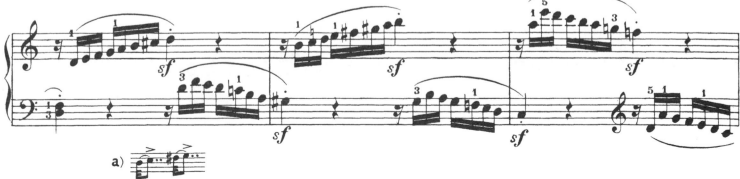

a)

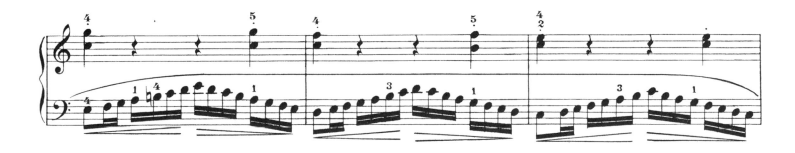

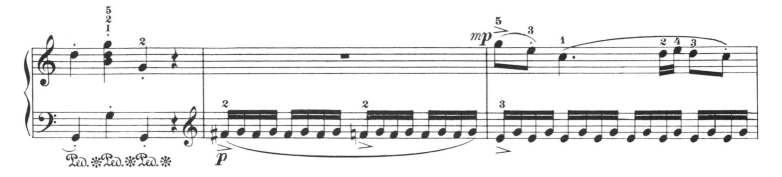

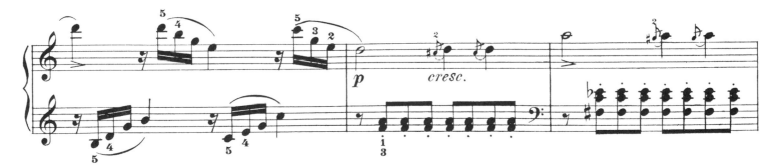

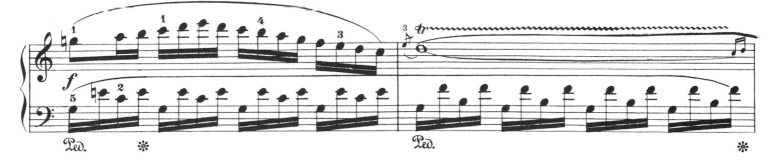

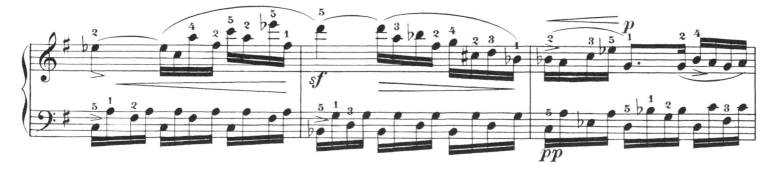

Rondo
Allegretto grazioso (♩ = 104)

PIANO SONATA
in B-flat Major

Edited, revised and fingered by
Richard Epstein

Wolfgang Amadeus Mozart
K. 333

Allegro (♩ = 116)

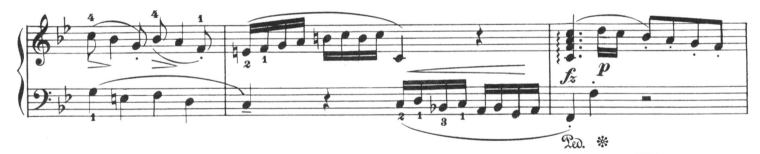

40

a)

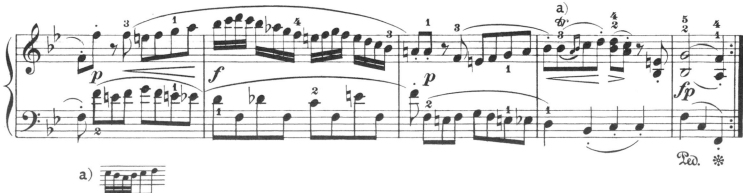

a)

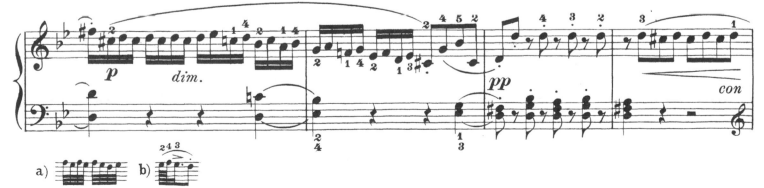

a)  b)

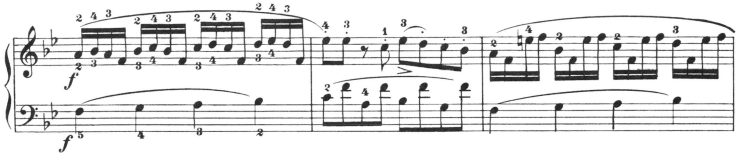

a)

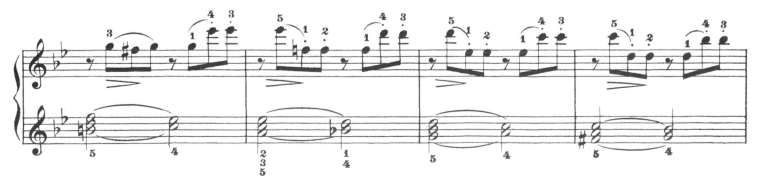

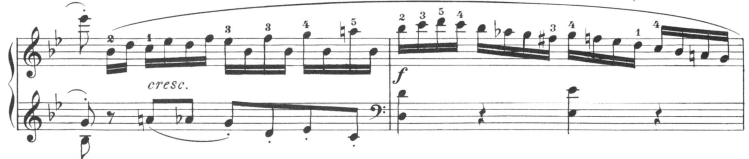

Andante cantabile (♩= 56)

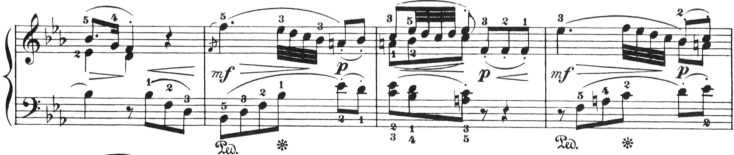

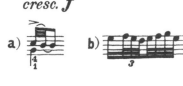

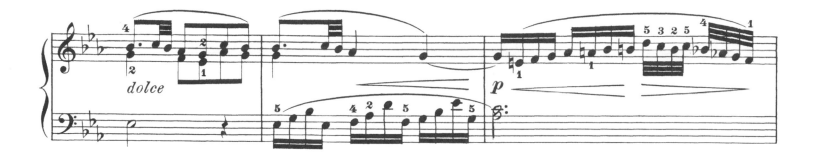

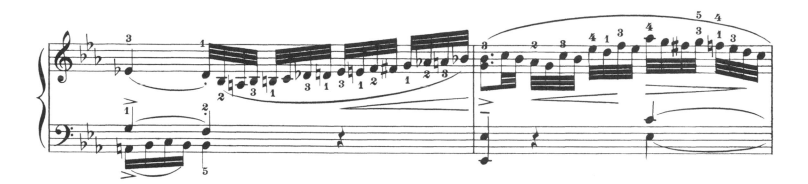

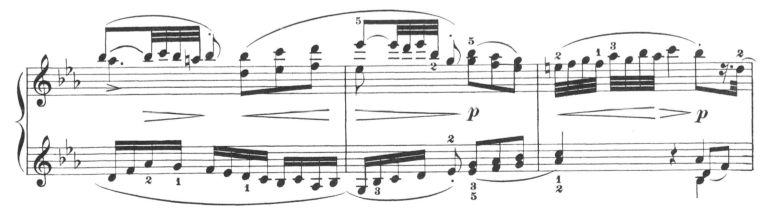

Allegretto grazioso ($\quarternote$ = 138)

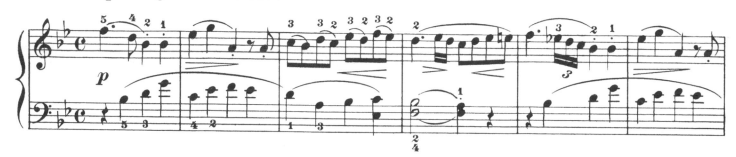

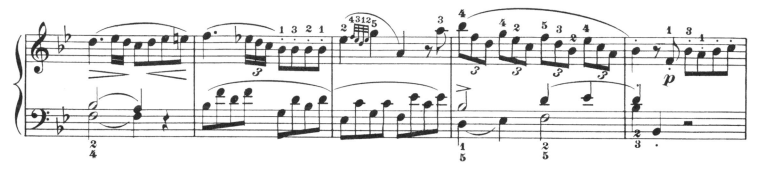

a)

52

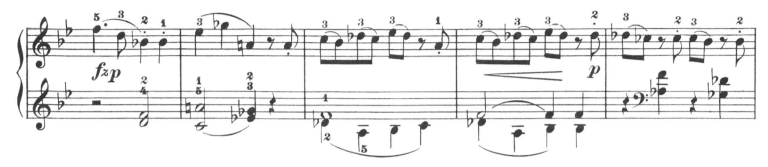

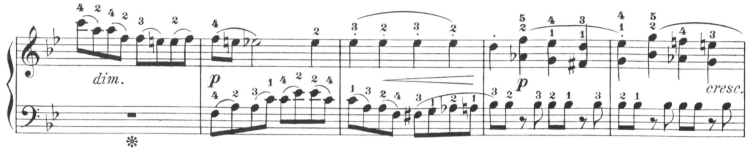

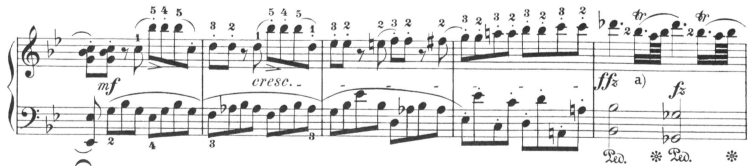

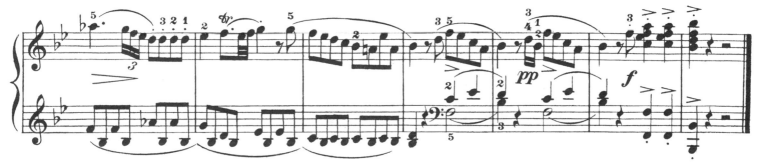

SONATINA
in C Major

Wolfgang Amadeus Mozart

Edited, revised and fingered by
Richard Epstein

Allegro

Menuetto

Allegretto

Trio

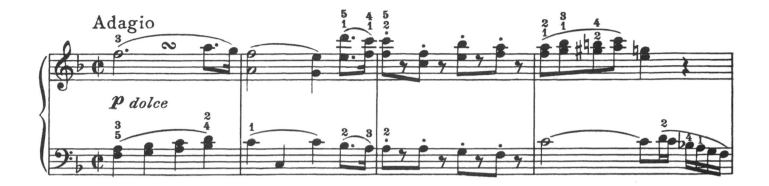

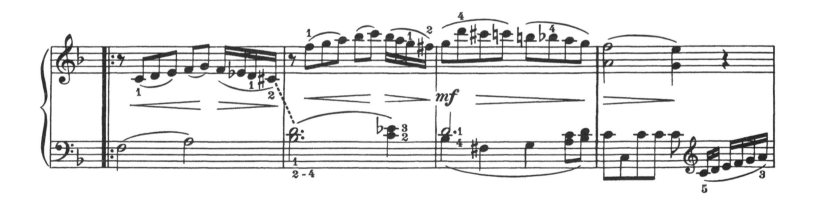

64

Rondo

Allegretto

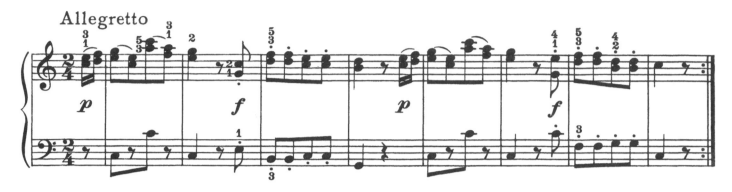

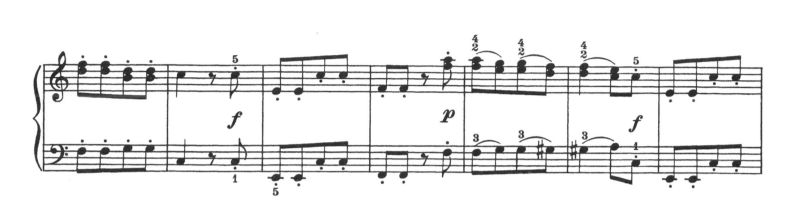

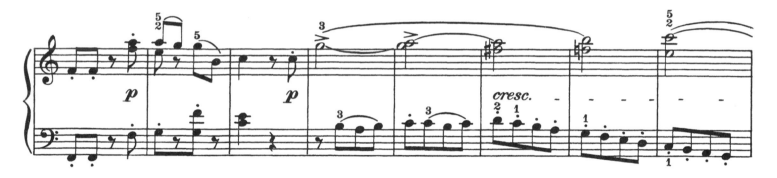

PIANO SONATA
in C Major

Wolfgang Amadeus Mozart
K. 309

Edited, revised and fingered by
Richard Epstein

Allegro con spirito (♩=144)

a) and **b**) A short trill, commencing on the principal
note.

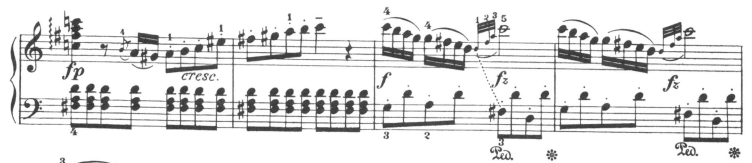

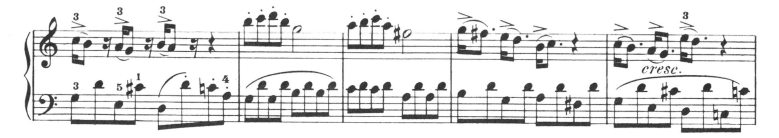

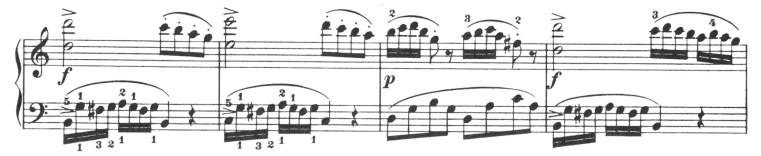

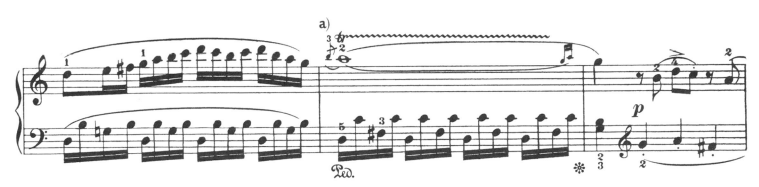

a) Play six notes on every quarter-note (crotchet).

b)

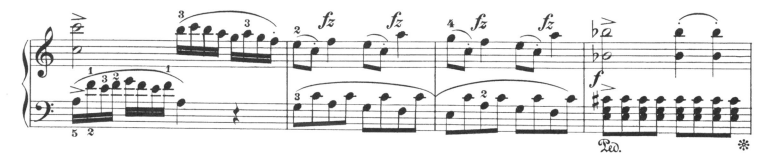

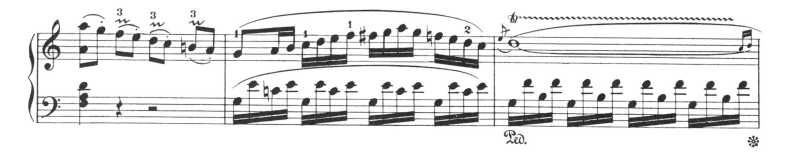

Andante un poco adagio (♩ = 50)

a)

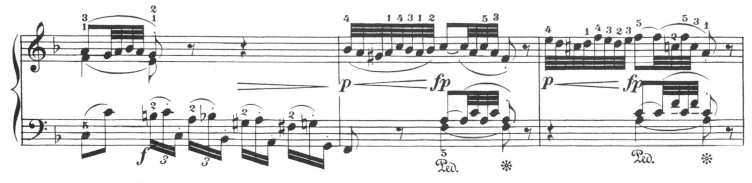

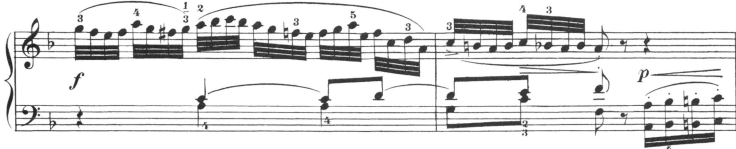

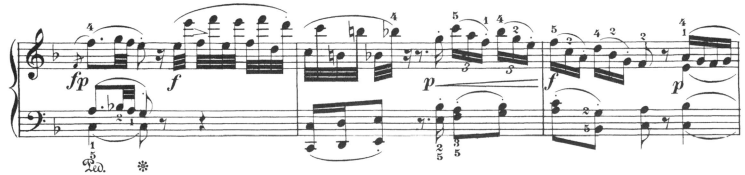

Rondo
Allegretto grazioso ($\quarternote$=88)

a)

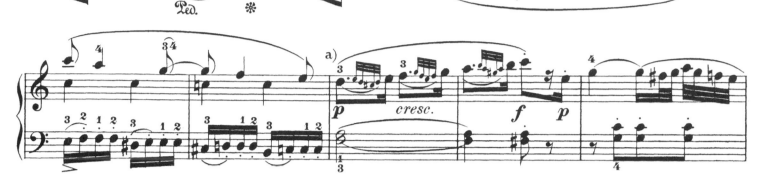

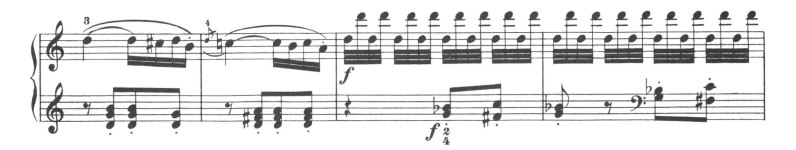

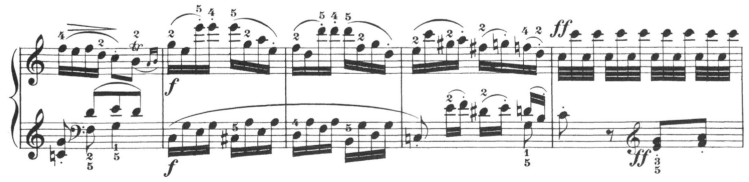

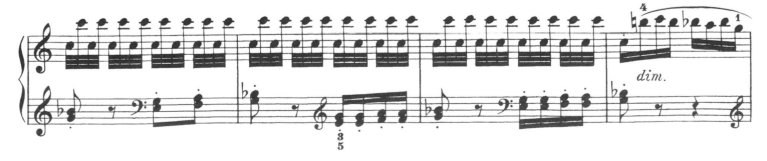

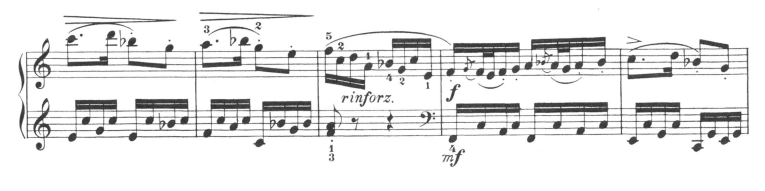

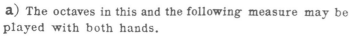

a) The octaves in this and the following measure may be
played with both hands.

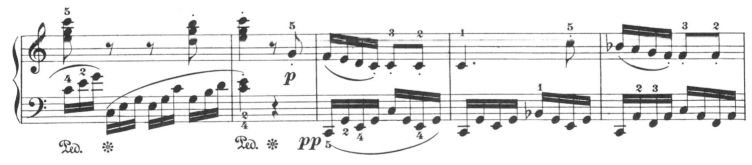

FANTASIA
in D minor

Wolfgang Amadeus Mozart
K. 397

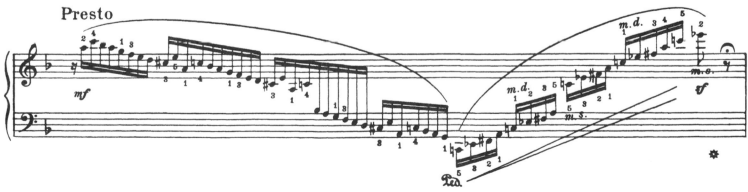

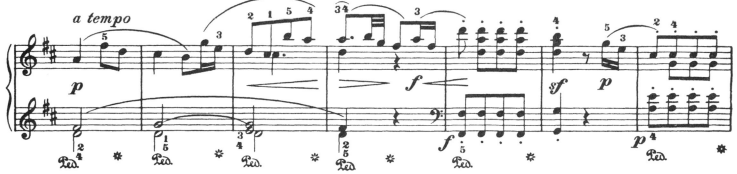

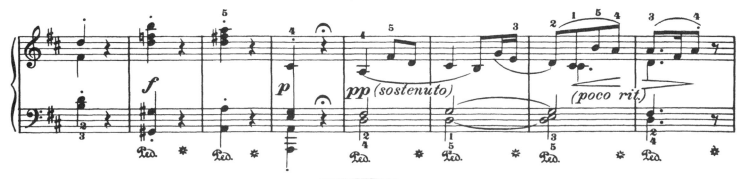

PIANO SONATA
in A minor

Edited, revised and fingered by
Richard Epstein

Wolfgang Amadeus Mozart
K. 310

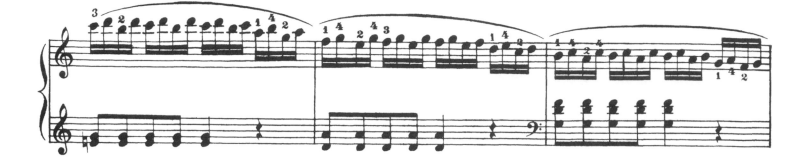

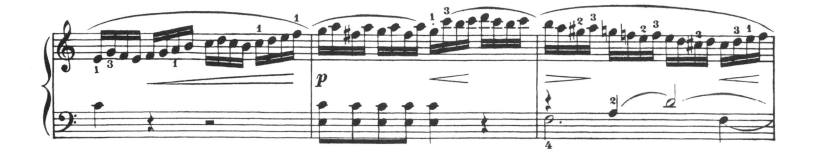

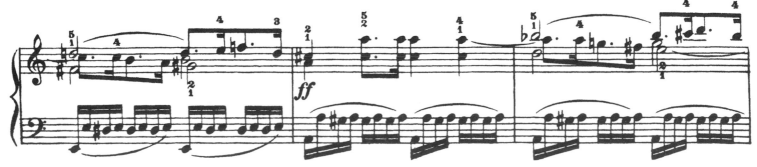

a)

Andante cantabile con espressione (♩=96)

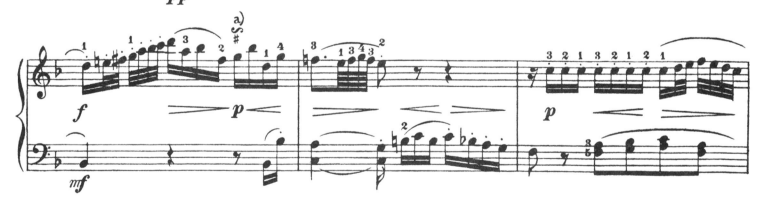

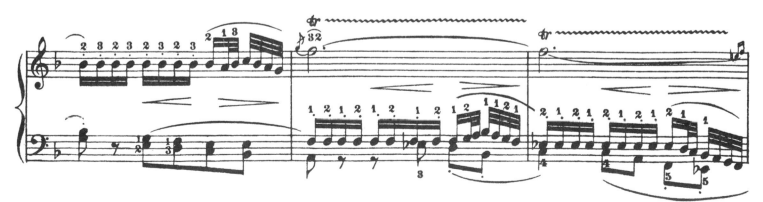

a)

Presto (♩=92)

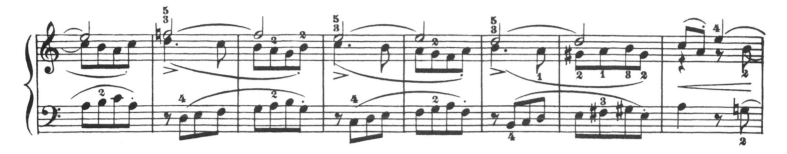

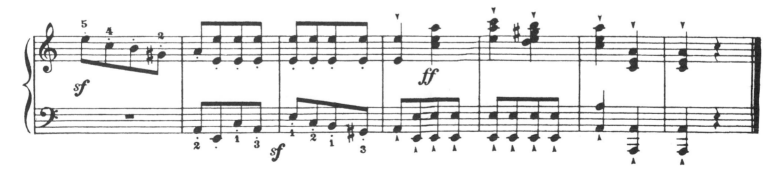

PIANO SONATA
in A Major

Edited, revised and fingered by
Richard Epstein

Wolfgang Amadeus Mozart
K. 331

Tema
Andante grazioso (♪ = 120)

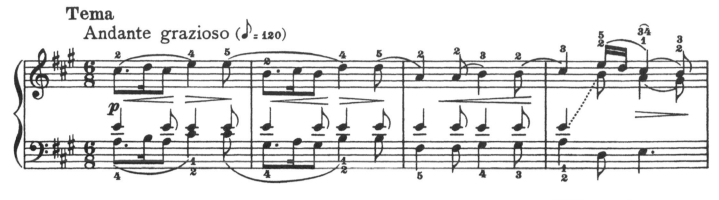

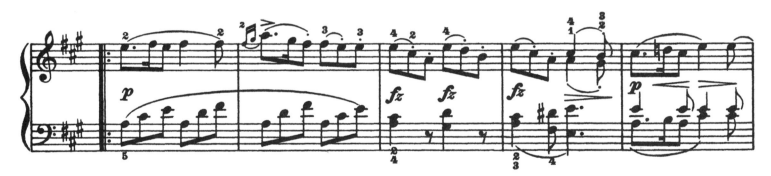

Var. I

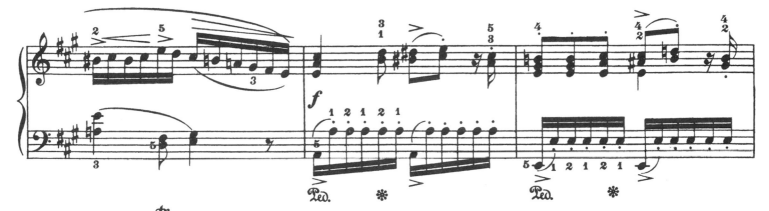

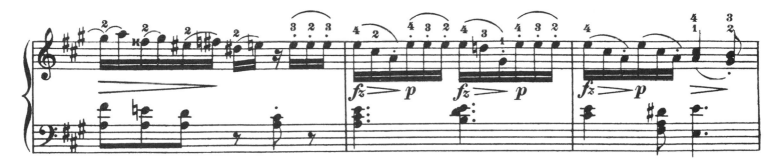

Var. III (♪ = 112)
Minore

Var. IV (♪ = 120)

Maggiore

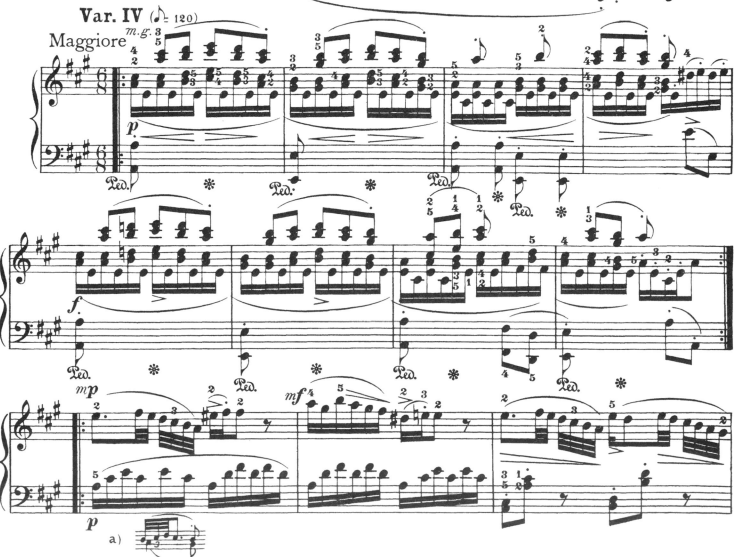

Var. V

Adagio (♪ = 60)

a)

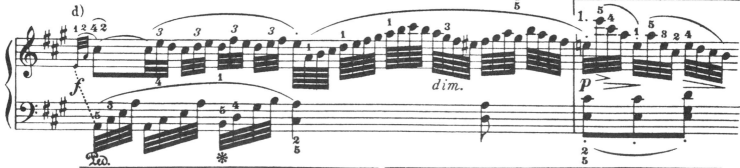

Var. VI
Allegro (♩ = 116)

a) The C sharp must enter with the bass note of
the left hand.

Menuetto ($\quad = 116$)

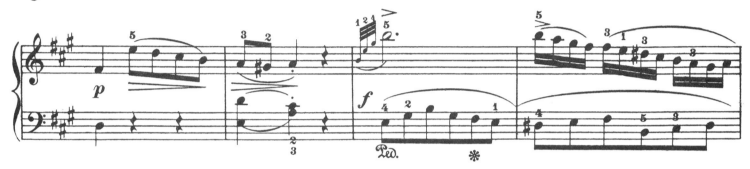

Trio

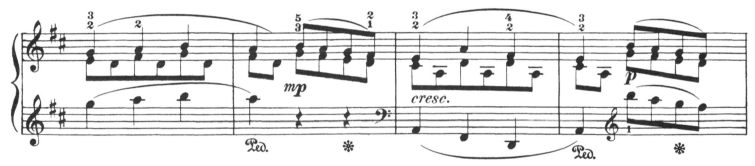

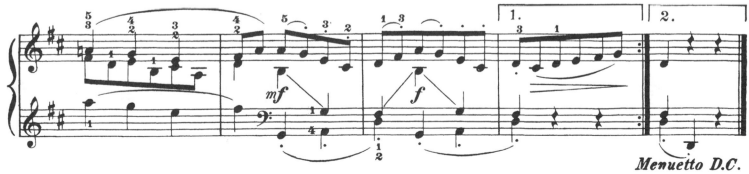

Menuetto D.C.

Alla turca
Allegretto (♩ = 126)   Rondo

a)

b) Play the first A in the bass with the C sharp in the
right hand.

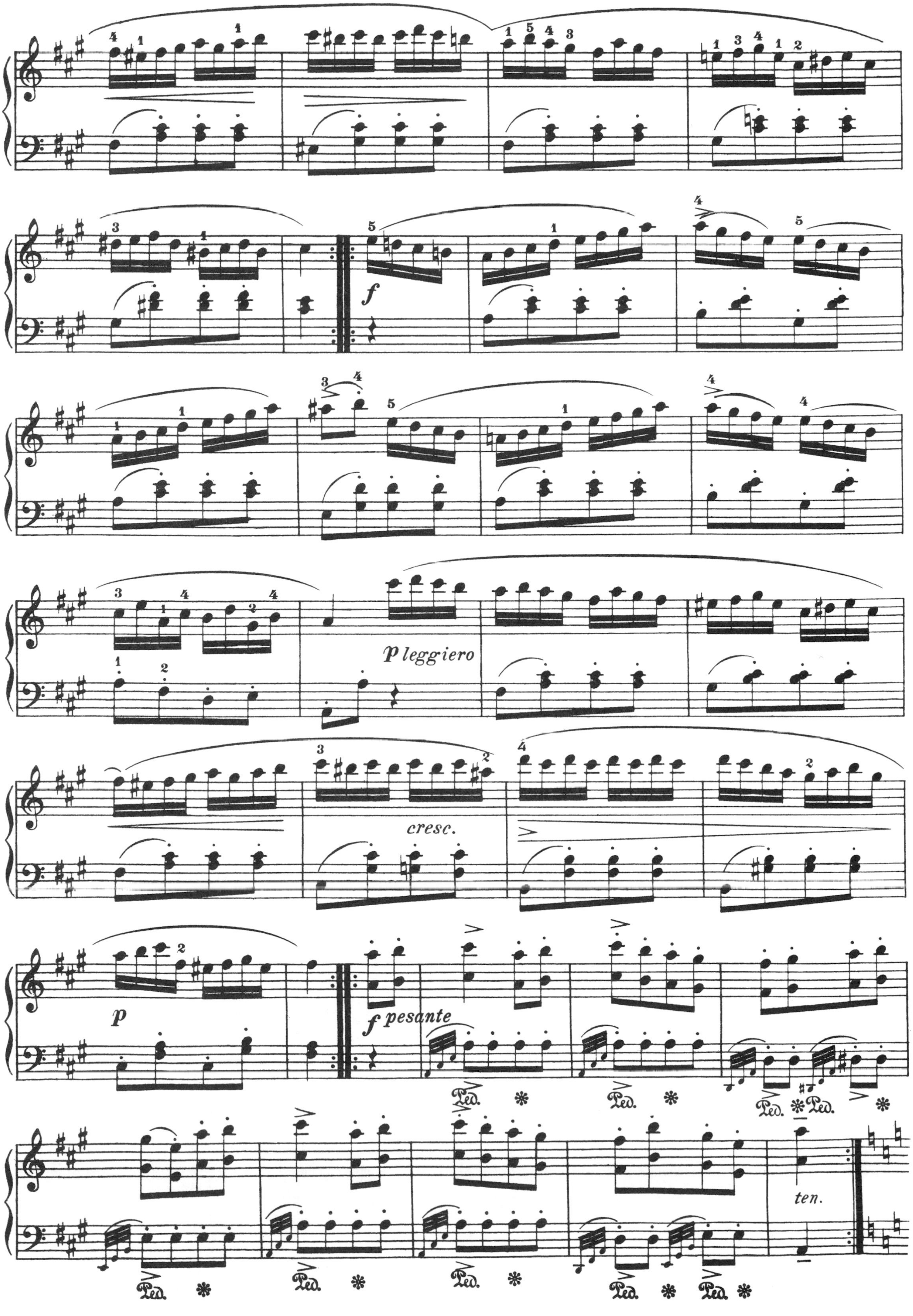
f
p leggiero
cresc.
p
f pesante
Ped.
ten.

124

a) Play the four notes in either hand simultaneously.

b)

FANTASIA AND SONATA
in C minor

Edited, revised and fingered by
Richard Epstein

Fantasia

Wolfgang Amadeus Mozart
K. 475 and 457

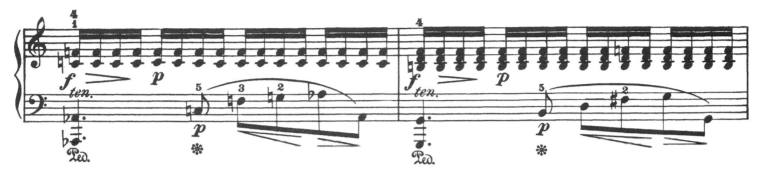

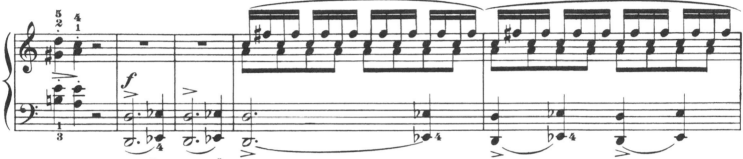

130

a)  b) The 2nd, 4th, 6th, and 8th notes in this measure may be played with the left hand.

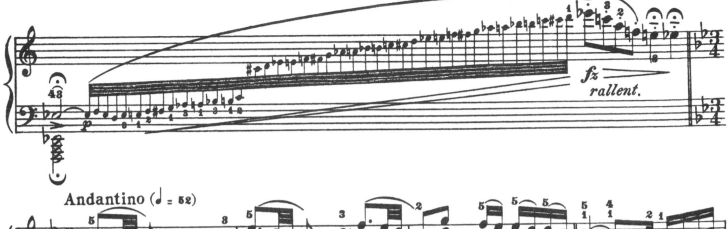

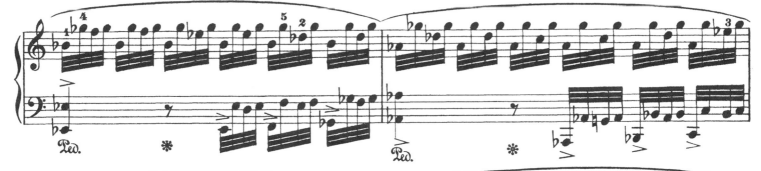

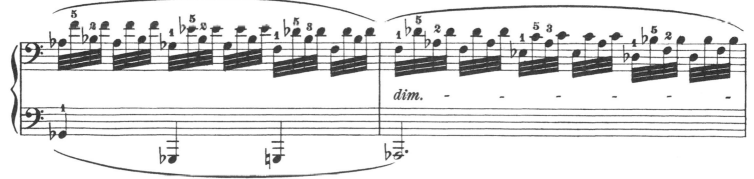

Sonata

a) The 2nd, 4th and 6th notes, etc., in this passage
may be played with the right hand.

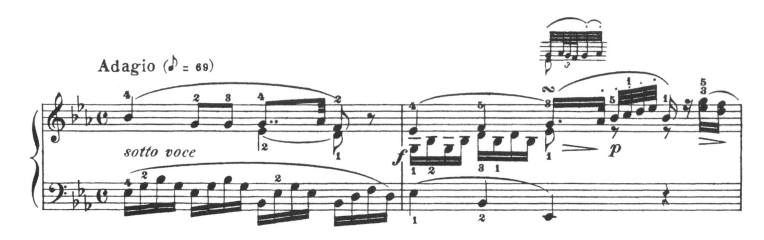

Adagio (♪ = 69)

sotto voce

cresc. *f* *p* *cresc.*

a)

f *p* *cresc.* *f* *p*

cresc. *f* *p* *p* *p*

Ped. ✳

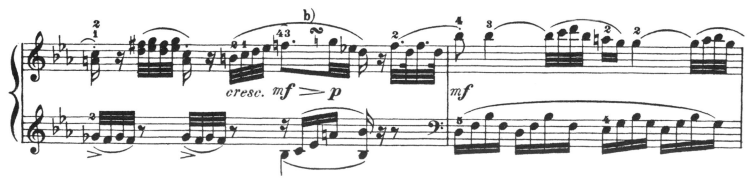

b)

cresc. *mf* *p* *mf*

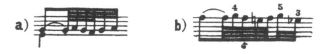

a)　　　　　b)

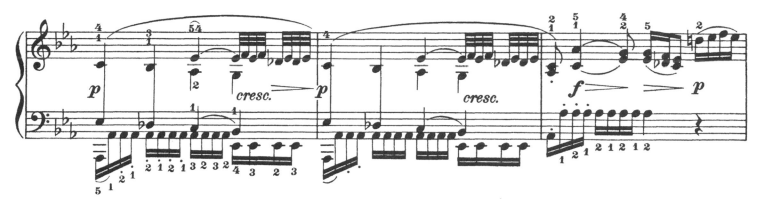

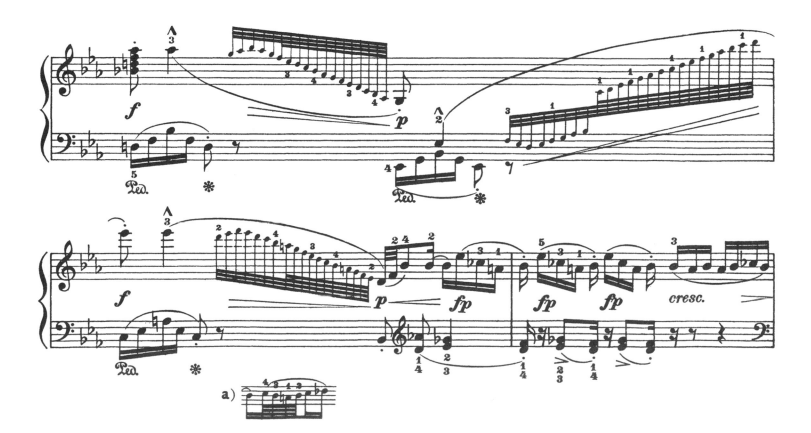

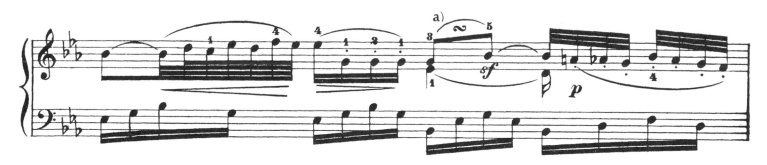

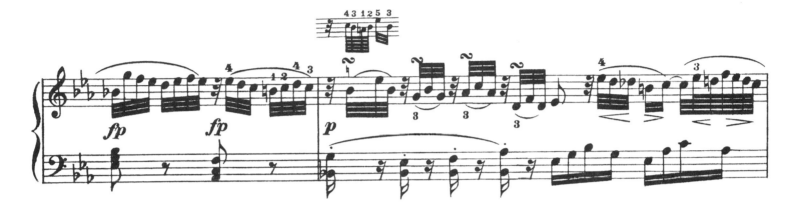

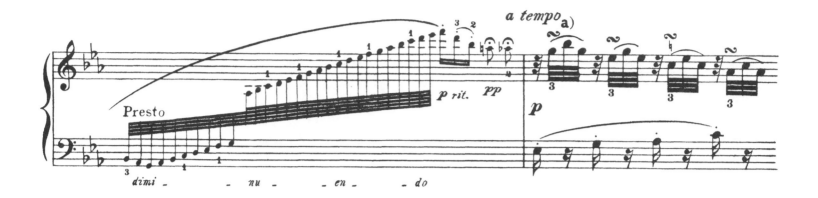

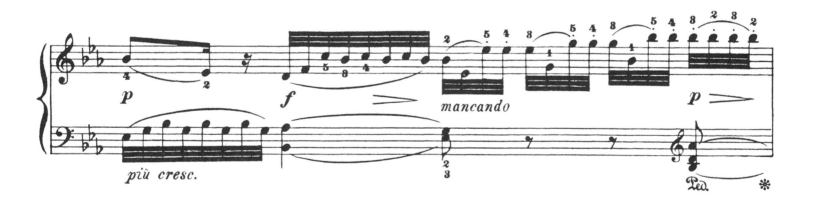

a)

Allegro assai (♩.=66)

EIGHT VARIATIONS

on "Laat Ons Juichen" by Christian Ernst Graaf

Wolfgang Amadeus Mozart

K. 24

VAR.II

VAR.III

VAR. IV

VAR. V

VAR. VI

VAR. VII
Adagio

VAR. VIII
Tempo I

legato

TWELVE VARIATIONS

on "Ah, vous dirai-je, Maman"

Wolfgang Amadeus Mozart

K. 265

(Moderato)

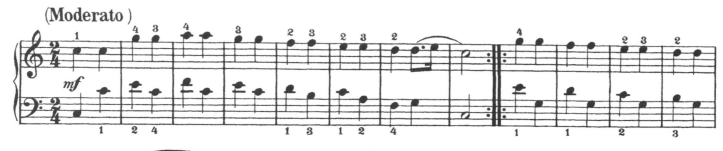

VAR. I

VAR. II

VAR.III

VAR.IV

VAR. V

VAR. VI

VAR.VII

VAR.VIII
Minore

VAR.IX
Maggiore

VAR.X

VAR.XI
Adagio